my first
SOCCER
BOOK

my first

SOCCER BOOK

learn how to play like a champion
with this fun guide to soccer:

- tackling
- shooting
- tricks
- tactics

Dominic Bliss

CICO kidz

Thank you to soccer dad and coach Charles Howgego for his help in preparing this book.

Published in 2015 by CICO Books
an imprint of Ryland Peters & Small Ltd
341 E 116th St, New York, NY 10029

www.rylandpeters.com

10 9 8 7 6 5 4 3 2 1

A CIP catalog record for this book is available from the Library of Congress.

ISBN: 978 1 78249 255 9

Printed in China

Editor: Katie Hardwicke
Series consultant: Susan Akass
Designer: Alison Fenton
Illustrator: Rachel Boulton
Character illustrations: Hannah George

In-house editor: Anna Galkina
In-house designer: Fahema Khanam
Art director: Sally Powell
Production manager: Gordana Simakovic
Publishing manager: Penny Craig
Publisher: Cindy Richards

The author and the publishers cannot accept any legal responsibility for any personal injury to children arising from the advice and activities outlined in this book. Every care has been taken to provide safety advice where needed. In particular, the handspring throw-in on page 56 and the overhead kick on pages 90—91 are tricky and potentially very dangerous. Do not attempt them unless you are a very experienced player and you are being supervised by a qualified coach.

Contents

Introduction

The whistle's gone and it's time for kick-off. Welcome to *My First Soccer Book*— a chance for you to learn everything you need to know about "the beautiful game".

Kids all across the planet love soccer. There's not one country on earth where they don't play it. That's because it's easy to learn, fun to play, and all you need is a soccer ball. You can play it in the park, in the street, on the beach, anywhere. And it's a sport as much for girls as for boys. In fact, more girls are playing soccer now than ever before.

In *My First Soccer Book* there are four chapters. First off, in Get Started, you'll learn about all the kit you need, the rules of the game, the different positions, and how to warm up properly.

Chapter Two will teach you all the basic skills you need to play: how to pass the ball to your team-mates, how to control the ball, how to tackle, dribble, shoot at goal, how to take corner kicks, throw-ins, free kicks, and penalties. Practice these and you'll be scoring goals in no time.

In Chapter Three you'll find out all about trickier skills like heading the ball, volleying, trick shots, and goalkeeping. There's also a section on practice drills, which you can use in training sessions with your friends

Finally, Chapter Four tells you all about how to make sure your team can begin winning games! Learn about team formations and attacking and defending tactics. Then there's a quiz to test how well you know your soccer rules.

What are you waiting for? Put on your boots, get out there, and play!

Soccer speak

Sometimes when playing or training for soccer, you'll come across words and phrases that you may not have heard before. Here's a quick guide to some special soccer words.

Clearance
A ball that is kicked away from the goal, out of the danger area.

Defenders
Players who play mainly at the back of their half, defending the goal.

Feinting
Pretending to turn one way before you actually turn the other way.

Formations
The way the players line up at the start of a match.

Hat-trick
When a player scores three goals in a match.

Intercept
When players steal the ball just as it's being passed between two players on the other team.

Into touch
Out of play, the other side of the touch line.

Marker
A player who shadows an opponent, staying close to him at all times.

Marking
Shadowing an opponent, staying close to him at all times.

Midfielders
Players who play between their defenders at the back of the pitch and their attackers at the front of the pitch.

Opposition
The other team.

Penalty
A free kick at goal from the penalty spot, with just the goalkeeper defending.

Stoppage
Time added to the end of the match to cover when play has stopped for injuries, or when there are delays in play.

Strikers
The players at the front of the pitch who often take shots at the other team's goal.

Throw-in
When players re-start the game by throwing the ball in from the touch lines.

Touch lines
These are the lines that mark the sides of the pitch.

Volley
When players kick the ball without controlling it or letting it bounce first.

Wingers
Players who run up and down the side of the pitch, crossing the ball into the center.

Wings
The sides of the pitch.

Training levels

Level 1
These soccer moves are simple and quick to learn

Level 2
These skills are a little more challenging and will get better with practice

Level 3
These skills need lots of practice and need you to be really fit and focused

chapter 1
Get started

What kit do I need?

Look at professional soccer players and you'll always see them dressed immaculately in their team kit. This shows their team-mates and the opposition that they're really serious about their sport.

The ball Make sure the soccer ball you're using is a proper one, made of synthetic leather. (The more expensive balls will have a FIFA logo on them.) You can buy really cheap balls in some stores but they won't have a true flight when you kick them and they won't last very long. Keep the ball well inflated—ask an adult to help you check the pressure and inflate the ball with a bicycle pump and ball valve needle if it needs it (see box).

Normally, the youngest players (under eight years old) use a size-3 ball, while junior players up to the age of 12 use a size-4 ball. Teenagers and grown-ups use a size-5 ball.

Keeping the ball inflated

If you don't keep your soccer ball inflated, it will get squashy and won't fly through the air properly when you kick it. Pumping it up is easy but you'll need a bicycle pump and a ball valve needle. Both are available from sporting goods stores.

1 Screw the ball valve needle into the valve on your pump.

2 Now find the valve on the soccer ball (a tiny, rubber hole). Dip the needle in some water before you push it gently into the valve.

3 Now pump up the ball. Keep checking it as you're pumping so that it's firm but not too hard. Most soccer balls should be inflated to between 6 and 8 psi (pounds per square inch).

Shirt

Shorts

Socks with shin guards

Boots

The clothes It's good for junior players to get into the habit, right from the start, of wearing the correct kit and using the correct equipment. You don't need to buy expensive kit to look smart.

Soccer boots Since you'll be running around for a long time in your soccer boots, it's worth spending money on a good brand. Leather will give you the best feel on the ball, but it needs regular cleaning and polishing. Think about the surface you'll be playing on—wet grass, dry grass, or artificial grass—so that you choose the correct studs or blades to get maximum grip. If you play on damp grass without studs or blades, you'll be sliding all over the place.

Tip

Always wear your soccer socks when trying on new boots to make sure you get the right size.

Socks Socks need to be pulled up to below your knees so that you can tuck shin guards inside them. Keep your socks up using special sock tape.

Shin guards The first time someone accidentally (or maybe on purpose!) kicks you in the shins, you'll wish you'd been wearing some shin guards. Some guards simply slot into your socks while others are strapped around your calves and also protect your ankles.

Shirts and shorts Once you join a team you'll wear the official team kit. But before then it's good to wear shirts and shorts designed specifically for soccer. Tucking your shirt into your shorts not only looks good but, more importantly, also gives the opposition less material to grab hold of. The goalkeeper's kit will be more padded and a different color to the rest of the team.

Goalkeeping gloves Goalies need protective gloves because they use their hands so much. The palm is extra-grippy while the back of the glove protects your hand and fingers.

Kit bag Keep all your kit together in a special bag so that it's ready when it's time for soccer practice or a match. A boot bag is a good idea, too, to keep the studs out of harm's way, and to stop dirt (mud) from getting on your clothes. Always clean your boots after playing and wash your clothes straight after a game.

Where can I play soccer?

The surface where you play soccer is known as the field, or pitch. The markings are an important part of the game and rules. Learn the names of the different lines and boxes and get to know your way round the pitch so that it becomes second nature to you.

Corner flag

Goal line   Goal

Goal area

Corner arc

Penalty spot

Penalty area

Penalty arc

Touch line
(or sideline)

Halfway line

Center spot

Center circle

Penalty area

Goal area

Goal

Goal line

There is no standard size for a soccer field, but a professional pitch is normally 115 yd (105 m) long and 74 yd (68 m) wide. Kids' pitches are much smaller than grown-up's pitches. Pitches are generally made of turf, or grass, but some pitches are made from artificial grass or even rubber chippings.

Center circle At the start of each half, and after every goal, there is a kick-off. Place the ball on the center spot for this. Players from the other team cannot enter the center circle until the ball has been played.

Halfway line This splits the field into two equal halves. Players must stay in their half of the pitch before a kick-off.

Goal Regular soccer goals are eight yards (7.32 m) wide and eight feet (2.44 m) high. On junior soccer pitches they are much smaller.

The goal line is the back boundary of the pitch. The goal area is the small box around the mouth of the goal.

Penalty area This is the larger box around the outside of the goal area—within the penalty area the goalkeeper is allowed to use his hands. If defenders commit a foul inside the penalty area the referee might award a penalty. Penalty kicks are taken from the penalty spot. During a penalty kick, only the penalty kicker and the opposition's goalkeeper are allowed inside the penalty area.

Penalty arc In addition to standing outside the penalty area, other players must be at least ten yards (9.14 m) from the penalty spot when a penalty is being taken. The penalty arc marks this distance —anyone inside the arc is too close to the ball.

Touch line The soccer field is a rectangular shape and the touch lines are the long lines along each side of the pitch. If the ball crosses the touch line it is put back into play with a "throw-in" (see page 54).

Corner flags and arcs On a regular soccer field there should be a flag in each corner. When players take a corner kick they must place the ball inside the corner arc.

Anyone for a game?

Of course, you don't need a proper soccer field to enjoy a game. The great thing about this sport is that you can play pretty much anywhere—in the park, in your back yard, on a quiet street (watch out for road users and pedestrians), or on the beach. Kids in Brazil often play soccer on the beach more than they do on grass.

You don't need a proper goal either—cones, bags, or sweaters will do for goalposts. Although a proper soccer match has two teams of 11 players, it's fine to play with much smaller teams.

The different positions

There are 11 players on a professional soccer team, split into a goalkeeper, defenders, midfielders, and attackers. These are known as positions and when you first start playing you won't be sure which position you enjoy most or which you're best at. This is something you'll later come to realize as you learn the game. Remember that every position is important for the team. It's well worth trying out the different positions to see which one you like most.

Tip

You don't need 11 people on each team to play a game of soccer, you can play smaller games with as few as five players on each team.

It's perfectly normal to start off in one position when you're very young but switch to another position when you get a bit older. Not everyone knows exactly which position they want to play in right from the start.

Goalkeeper Goalkeepers are the only players allowed to use their hands during play. They must use every skill possible—diving, jumping, catching the ball, deflecting the ball—to stop the other team scoring. They must also learn to kick well. The world's greatest ever goalkeepers—like Germany's Oliver Kahn, Spain's Iker Casillas, Denmark's Peter Schmeichel, and Italy's Gianluigi Buffon—are really strong in all these areas.

Defenders Defenders spend much of their time close to their own goal, marking the other team's attackers, and tackling them when they get too close. They need to work really closely with the goalkeeper. Two of the greatest ever soccer defenders are Germany's Franz Beckenbauer and Itay's Paolo Maldini.

Midfielders Playing in between the defenders and attackers, these players often cover more of the pitch than other players. They must help the defenders and create chances for the attackers. Long passing skills (being able to kick the ball a long distance to another player on your team) are especially important. Argentina's Diego Maradona, Holland's Johan Cruyff, Northern Ireland's George Best, and France's Zinedine Zidane, were all brilliant midfielders.

Attackers The main job of the attackers is to shoot and score goals. They often need to move very fast. Heading skills are crucial, too. Some attackers (called wingers) play on the wings (the sides of the pitch), so they need to learn how to cross the ball—kicking the ball across to another player on your team. Other attackers (called strikers) play in the center, so they need to shoot at goal. There have been so many famous soccer strikers over the years but nearly everyone agrees Brazil's Pelé was the best ever.

Referee

The referee makes sure all the players obey the rules of soccer. He or she is in charge and, using their whistle to stop play, they will award free kicks, penalties, yellow cards, and red cards when players break the rules. A referee for a professional game of soccer must be qualified and will often be an adult or an older youth who has passed the referee tests.

Rules of the game

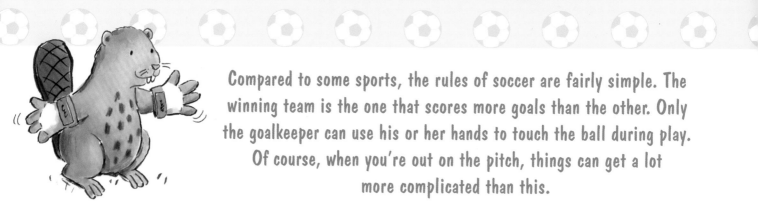

Compared to some sports, the rules of soccer are fairly simple. The winning team is the one that scores more goals than the other. Only the goalkeeper can use his or her hands to touch the ball during play. Of course, when you're out on the pitch, things can get a lot more complicated than this.

Soccer basics

● In a proper soccer match there are 11 players on each team.

● The amount of time a grown-ups' soccer match is played is broken into two periods of 45 minutes each—the first half and the second half. The total amount of time for a game is 1 hour and 30 minutes, plus 15 minutes for half-time, plus any extra time to make up for stoppage (see page 7).

● Before the start of a match, a coin is tossed. The team captain that wins the toss decides which goal his or her team will attack in the first half of the match. The other team then takes the kick-off to start the

match once the referee has blown his whistle. In the second half the teams swap ends. The team that originally won the coin toss takes the kick-off at the start of the second half. If extra time is played another coin toss is used at the beginning of this period.

● Players kick off from the center spot at the start of both halves and after a goal is scored.

Corner kicks If a defending player is the last to touch the ball before it goes behind the goal line, then the attacking team is given a corner kick. Corner kicks must be taken from inside the corner arc.

Throw-ins If one player is the last to touch the ball before it goes past the touch line then the other team is given a throw-in.

Offside If it wasn't for the offside rule then attacking players could hang around near the other team's goal, waiting to score, without doing any work at all. (See opposite for an illustration of how the offside rule works.)

Players are offside if someone kicks the ball through to them and they are nearer to their opponents' goal line than both the ball and the second-last opponent. (The last opponent is usually, but not always, the goalkeeper).

Remember, you can't be offside if:
• you're in your own half of the pitch
• you're level with the second-last opponent
• you're level with the last two opponents
• you receive the ball directly from a goal kick, a throw-in, or a corner kick.

The offside rule may sound complicated but you'll soon learn exactly how it works.

Goals A goal is scored when the ball crosses the goal line between the goal posts and below the crossbar. But it must cross the line completely to count.

Passing back to the goalkeeper If defenders pass backward to their own goalkeeper, then the goalkeeper cannot use his or her hands to play the ball.

Goal kicks A kick is taken by the defending side (usually by the goalkeeper) from within their goal area after attackers send the ball over the goal line.

In this game red is attacking. The red player on the left is offside because he is in front of the second last opponent (the goal keeper is the last opponent) when the ball is kicked through to him.

May the best team win

Like any sport, soccer isn't just about winning. Manners and good sportsmanship are important, too.

• However heated a match gets, always keep your cool.

• Never argue with the referee.

• If another player fouls you, you should never retaliate.

The world's most famous players are often those with the best manners on the pitch. England player Gary Lineker was a great example of this. In all his years in action he never once received either a yellow or a red card. He was given FIFA's fair play award.

Fouls-breaking the rules

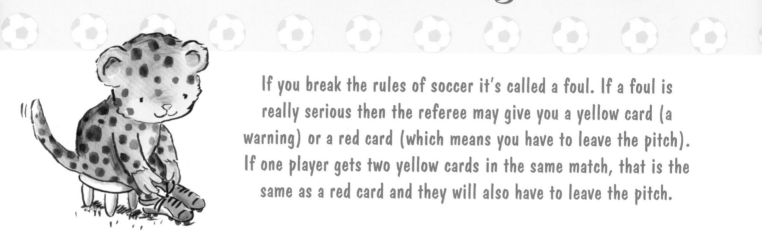

If you break the rules of soccer it's called a foul. If a foul is really serious then the referee may give you a yellow card (a warning) or a red card (which means you have to leave the pitch). If one player gets two yellow cards in the same match, that is the same as a red card and they will also have to leave the pitch.

Always listen to what the referee says, even if you think they are being too strict. Refereeing a soccer match, even at junior level, is not an easy job. The reason referees blow their whistle is because they want to make sure every match is fair and every player is safe.

Offences Soccer is a contact sport. When players are running, tackling, and jumping for the ball they often knock into each other. Every player needs to learn what's allowed and what isn't allowed.

Sometimes soccer players are reckless, which means they behave carelessly or dangerously. A referee will award a free kick if players recklessly kick, trip, strike, charge, jump at, or push an opponent. Or if they are reckless while tackling. Or if they hold an opponent's body or clothing. If you commit any of these offences inside your own penalty area, a penalty kick will be given to the other team.

Hand ball Only goalkeepers are allowed to touch the ball with their hands. A hand ball is when other players touch the ball with their hands and then the opposing team gets a free kick. If a defender uses his or her hands in the penalty area to stop a shot on goal, they may be given a red card and a penalty will be awarded against them.

Back passes to the goalkeeper Goalkeepers are not allowed to touch the ball with their hands if one of their team-mates passes back to them. The same rule applies if one of their team-mates throws the ball to them from a throw-in.

Six-second rule Once goalkeepers pick up the ball they have six seconds before they have to release it back into play.

Red cards Some offences are so bad that players immediately get a red card and have to leave the pitch. These include serious foul play, violence, spitting, or using bad language.

Uruguayan player Luis Suarez has been punished many times for really bad behavior on the pitch.

Getting ready to play—warm-ups

It's really important to warm up and stretch your body before you start playing, especially if it's cold. Not only will you move better right from the start of the match, but you're also less likely to get an injury because your muscles will be more flexible.

Jogging Start off with a gentle jog around the edge of the pitch, just to warm up your muscles.

Drink some water

A long soccer match can really test your body. Make sure you've drunk enough water before you start.

Star jumps Star jumps are a great way to warm up your legs and your arms. Do around 20.

Kick movements You're going to be doing a lot of kicking during the match so it's a good idea to practice the movement by swinging your leg forward to back, pretending to kick a ball.

Quadriceps Your quadriceps is the muscle at the front of your upper thigh. Stretch it by folding your lower leg behind you and up to your backside, holding the top of your foot. Gently stretch the muscle for 20 seconds, rest, and repeat twice more. Do this for three times on both legs.

Hamstrings Hamstring is the name for the tendons and muscles at the back of your thigh. Lots of professional soccer players injure their hamstrings so it's really sensible to make sure they are warmed up properly. Sit on the ground with one leg stretched out in front of you. Lean forward and place your hands right down your leg toward your ankle. Gently stretch the muscles for 20 seconds, rest, and repeat twice more. Do this three times on both legs.

Warm down

At the end of a match professional soccer players also warm down their muscles to avoid injury and stiffness. Do similar jogging and stretches as you did before the match.

Groin These are the muscles where your thighs join your body. Sit down on the ground with the soles of your feet pressed together. Use your elbows to gently press your knees down toward the floor, stretching your groin muscles. Hold for 20 seconds and repeat three times.

Calf muscle This is the muscle at the back of your lower leg. To stretch it, stand against a wall with one foot forward, one foot back. Push against the wall, keeping your back foot flat on the ground. Gently stretch your calf muscle in your back leg for 20 seconds, rest, and repeat twice more. Do this three times on both legs.

Sprints You're going to be doing a lot of running during a soccer match, much of it at top speed. It's good to do some short sprints in the warm-up so that your body is used to the fast movements before the match starts.

Kicking and heading You should always do some real kicking and heading before the match starts so that your body and mind are ready for competitive play. Practice the type of ball play that you'll be doing during the match. So a winger should practice a few crosses while a striker should practice shooting and heading at goal. A goalkeeper should practice saving shots on goal.

chapter 2
Passing, kicking, & more

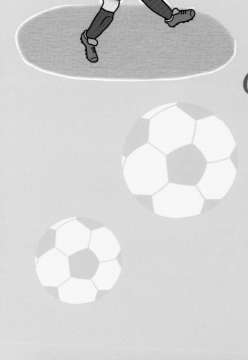

Push passing

Sometimes called side-foot passing, push passing is the simplest way to pass the ball over a short distance to one of your team-mates. Using the side of your foot, you stroke the ball firmly along the ground. It's easy to aim and control the ball because you use the largest part of your foot. But it's difficult to generate much power, so the push pass isn't good for long passes.

 1 Look around you and decide which team-mate you're going to kick the ball to.

 2 Position your non-kicking foot on one side of the ball, very close to it, pointing in the direction you want the ball to go. Keep watching the ball closely. Use your arms to keep yourself balanced.

3 Bring your head and body directly above the ball as you swing your kicking leg toward it. Make sure when you strike the ball that your foot is turned sideways so the inside of your foot hits the middle of the ball squarely, and that your ankle is firm.

4 Follow right through the middle of the ball with your kicking leg and keep watching the ball as it moves toward your team-mate.

Long kicks

Sometimes you need to pass the ball to a team-mate a long way down the pitch. Push passing won't be powerful enough. What you need is a much stronger pass, using the front of your foot to kick the ball. These kinds of passes are trickier to control and you'll have to practice them a lot before you become accurate.

1 Look around you and decide which team-mate you're going to kick the ball to. It's good if that team-mate isn't marked, or shadowed, by an opponent. Remember, if there are opponents between you and your team-mate, they may intercept the ball.

Tip

If you want the ball to go up in the air, you need to place your non-kicking foot to the side but slightly behind the ball and then lean back slightly as you kick the ball.

Bend the ball

It's actually quite easy to make your long kicks swerve instead of going straight.

• To bend kicks left, strike the right side of the ball with the left side of the toes on your right foot.

• To bend kicks right, strike the left side of the ball with the right side of the toes on your right foot.

• Kicking the ball just off-center will give you more power and less swerve.

• Kicking the ball on the edge will give you more swerve and less power.

England player David Beckham used to be one of the best players in the world at bending the ball like this. He scored many classic goals from free kicks that swerved around the goalkeeper.

2 You'll need to take a few steps before you kick the ball so you get momentum and power. Keep watching the ball as you step toward it, otherwise you'll kick it in the wrong direction.

Tip

Don't use the end of your toes to kick the ball hard. It's really tricky to control the ball if you kick it like this. But occasionally, if the ball is running away from you and you need to stretch out far to kick it, you might find using the end of your toes is the best thing to do.

3 Place your non-kicking foot on one side of the ball, very close to it, pointing in the direction you want the ball to go. Keep watching the ball closely. Use your arms to keep yourself balanced. At the same time, swing your kicking leg back, bending it slightly with your knee above the ball.

4 Swing your kicking leg firmly at the ball. Point your toes down toward the pitch and kick through the middle of the ball with your laces. Try to make the ball land in front of your team-mate's feet. This takes practice, especially if your team-mate is running at the time.

5 Follow right through with your kicking leg and keep watching the ball as it moves toward your team-mate.

Chipping

Sometimes you need to kick the ball over the heads of your opponents to a team-mate on the other side of them. If the ball doesn't fly high enough it will be intercepted and your team will lose possession. This is where a chip pass is needed.

1 Look beyond the opponents for the team-mate you want to chip the ball to. It's best if he or she isn't marked.

2 You need only a short run up for a chip because you're normally kicking it high but just a short distance.

3 Place your non-kicking foot close to the side of the ball. Swing your kicking foot back a short way.

4 Kick the bottom of the ball with a quick stabbing motion. This puts backspin on the ball and lets you scoop it upward over the head of your opponent. Good backspin will make the ball stop quickly once it lands the other side. There should be almost no follow-through with this kick.

Chip and win

Chipping is a great way to surprise the goalkeeper and score a goal. If a goalkeeper is coming toward you, away from his or her goal line, you can chip the ball over their head and into the net. They will be really annoyed but your team-mates will be delighted.

Controlling the ball

There's no point learning how to kick the ball if you don't also know how to control it when it comes to you. Sometimes the ball will come right to your feet, other times it will bounce high or land a distance away. You must learn how to control it and trap it using your feet, your legs, or your chest. Only then will you be able to pass it on safely to one of your team-mates.

Trap the ball on the ground One way to stop the ball is to trap it dead. You can do this either when it's rolling along the ground toward you (quite easy) or when it bounces at your feet (much trickier). In both cases, bring your foot down firmly on top of the ball, just in front of you, wedging it between your sole and the ground. Don't lift your foot too high or the ball will pass straight under it.

The only problem with trapping the ball like this is that you have to move your foot down and off the ball before you can pass it to a team-mate. This takes valuable time, especially if an opponent is coming in to tackle you.

Control with your feet As the ball comes toward you (either along the ground or in the air), use the side of your foot to take the pace (or speed) off of the ball. You do this by bringing your leg back slightly to cushion it to a stop (instead of stopping it dead). Use your arms to keep yourself balanced.

If the ball is in the air and you control it properly, it will then drop to the ground where you can use your foot to stop it moving.

Control with your thigh Often the ball will come to you at tummy height. Lift up your thigh and use it to take the pace (speed) off of the ball, bringing your thigh down and back slightly to cushion the ball (instead of stopping it dead). Keep your body and head above the ball, and use your arms to keep yourself balanced. The ball will then drop gently to your feet.

Control with your chest Sometimes the ball will come to you after bouncing really high. Often, the best way to control it is with your chest. Keep your elbows close to your sides and your forearms facing forward so that you don't accidentally touch the ball with your hands. Arch your back and lean back slightly. Use your chest to cushion the ball (instead of stopping it dead). If you then move your shoulders forward the ball will drop gently to your feet. Be careful the ball doesn't bounce up into your face.

Dribbling

Dribbling is when you run with the ball, using gentle taps and nudges with your feet to move it along the ground. You keep it close to your feet, where you can control it, at all times. If you have good speed, balance, and control, you can move long distances down the pitch without losing possession of the ball. Really skilled players can dribble the ball around defenders before shooting at goal.

1 You need to be aware of both the ball and the players around you. Most of the time you should be looking up for team members to pass to, and for opposing players to avoid. But every half-second or so you should glance down at the ball so you don't lose control of it.

2 Tap and nudge the ball gently with the inside or outside of your feet to keep it moving along. Use both feet so that you can easily switch directions if another player comes up to tackle you.

3 Make sure the ball rolls no more than a few feet (half a meter or so) away from you at any time. Otherwise opposing players could steal it from you.

4 Deception (tricking people) is an important skill when you're dribbling because it lets you dribble past players from the other team. If a defender runs toward you to make a tackle, drop your left shoulder, pretending that you're going to move to the left. Hopefully the defender will be tricked into moving the same way. At the last second you swerve to the right, around the defender, and then you dribble away from him. This is sometimes called feinting.

5 Even the world's best players get tackled when they're dribbling, and lose the ball. That's why you should always be ready to pass to one of your team-mates. It's often too risky to dribble when you're close to your own goal in case an opposing player tackles you and scores.

Tip

Here's a great way to practice your dribbling skills: set up a line of eight or ten cones on the pitch, with a few feet (half a meter or so) of space between each one. Now dribble the ball in a slalom around the cones. Start off at walking pace. As you get more confident and learn control and balance, you'll be able to dribble faster. But remember, cones don't move. Opposing players do!

Going the distance

Soccer players need to be really fit, especially if they're dribbling the ball over long distances. Professional players will run between five and eight miles during a match, sometimes with the ball, other times chasing it.

Argentina's Diego Maradona was one of the best dribblers the sport has ever seen. He could duck and weave around several defenders, and the goalkeeper, before shooting the ball into the back of the net. Another Argentinean player, Lionel Messi, is a great dribbler too.

Shooting

Many soccer players find shooting at goal is the most exciting part of the game—especially if you end up scoring. But it's not easy. There are defenders and a goalkeeper to kick past. And you may be running at top speed without a clear shot at the goal. Good soccer players need to be able to shoot with both feet.

1 Be sensible. You won't score a goal from halfway down the field (unless you're David Beckham!). You need to be close to the goal to have a chance of scoring— somewhere inside the penalty area or not too far outside it. And you need to have a clear shot with nothing between you and the goal, even if it's only a very small gap. Don't be greedy—if one of your team-mates has a better chance at scoring, pass it to them instead of shooting yourself.

2 If you're going to shoot, do it quickly before the defenders and goalkeeper have time to get into position.

3 If you have the option, aim for the corners of the goal. This will make it much more difficult for the goalkeeper to save your shot. Goalkeepers normally find it easier to stretch up to the top corners than they do to dive down to the bottom corners. But remember that shots to the corners can easily miss, or rebound off the goalposts.

4 Kick the ball as you would a normal kick (see push passes and long kicks on pages 28 and 30, and volleying on page 66)—with the side of your foot if it's a short distance to the goal, or with your laces, or the inside or outside of your toes, for longer shots.

5 Use your arms to keep yourself balanced. Keep watching the ball as you strike it. Keep your body and head above the ball throughout the kick.

6 Don't try to kick the ball too hard because you risk losing control and sending it wide or over the top of the crossbar. A soft, accurate shot on goal is often more effective than blasting the ball and risking sending it wide.

7 Swing your kicking leg right through the ball to give it extra pace and direction.

Hat-tricks

All soccer players love scoring goals and they are the most exciting part of soccer. Score three goals in one match and it's called a hat-trick.

In the professional game, Brazilian legends such as Roberto Carlos, Ronaldo, Eusebio, and Pelé have amazed fans with their shooting skills.

8 Be ready for a rebound. The ball might bounce back off of the goalposts, the crossbar, or the goalkeeper. You never know—you may be lucky and get a second chance to score.

Tackling

If the other team has possession of the ball, it's your job to tackle them and win the ball back for your team. Tackling is when soccer is at its liveliest. Since tackling involves bodily contact between two players, it's also when tempers run high, misunderstandings occur, or players get into trouble.

• Whenever you tackle another player, make sure it's a clean tackle by only playing the ball, not touching the other player's body. Otherwise you risk a free kick or even a card from the referee.

• You can tackle another player from the side, from the front, or from behind. But if you're tackling from behind, be extra careful you make contact only with the ball, not the player. A referee will often award a free kick for a tackle from behind because it can cause injuries.

• Keep your eye on the ball at all times during a tackle.

Block tackle The most common tackle is the block tackle. Usually you'll be facing your opponent as they come toward you. Place your non-tackling foot firmly on the ground to give yourself a solid base. Lean toward your opposing player and use the inside of your tackling foot to drive through the ball. If you have enough power and momentum you will come away from the tackle with the ball. Make sure you really commit yourself—be determined and confident—to the tackle.

Slide tackles This is when you slide, foot-first, at the ball while a player on the other team has possession of it. If you can, you should use your stronger kicking foot to make the tackle, with your other leg slightly bent as you slide in. When you do this, you will end up off your feet and on the ground.

Tip

A successful slide tackle will normally push the ball away from the player who had it. It won't win you possession, but it can stop an opponent from shooting at goal.

Slide tackles are risky for two reasons. Firstly, it's easy to miss the ball and foul the other player by mistake, by kicking them or pushing them for example. Secondly, because the tackler ends up on the ground, they will be out of the game for a few seconds. If you do a slide tackle, get back onto your feet as quickly as possible.

Corner kicks

When a defender or the goalkeeper is the last to touch the ball before it goes behind their own goal line, the attacking team is given a corner kick. Corners are a great chance for the attacking team to score because lots of their players can place themselves in the penalty area while one of their team kicks the ball to them from the corner flag. They can then kick or head the ball into the goal. The defending team must be really careful not to let in a goal.

1 The corner kick is taken from the corner on the side of the goal where the ball went behind the goal line.

2 Defenders must be at least 10 yd (9.1 m) away from the ball when a corner kick is taken.

3 Attacking players should try to get into a space where they aren't marked by defenders so they have the best chance to score. At the same time, defenders should try to mark the attacking players. There will be lots of jostling for position as the kick is taken.

4 The ball must be inside the corner arc before the player takes the corner kick.

5 Corner kickers should kick the ball the same way they would do on a long kick (see page 30). Quite often, corner kickers will use the inside of their toes to curve the ball toward the goal or away from the goal. If you're good enough at swerving the ball, you can score directly from a corner kick.

6 Corner kickers will normally try to kick the ball hard enough so that it passes somewhere inside or close to the goal area, at around head height. They have many options. They can aim for the near post, for the far post, for the center of the goal mouth, or for a player on their team who they see is unmarked.

Crosses

Crosses are a bit like corner kicks except that you are kicking the ball while it's moving. Most crosses are kicked from the wing into the penalty area. The important thing is to aim for one of your team-mates—don't just kick the ball anywhere. Look up before you make your cross, choose the player you're going to kick to, and try to place the ball on their head or just in front of them.

Free kicks

If the other team does a foul or breaks the rules of soccer, your team will be given a free kick. Depending on how serious the foul was, it might be a direct free kick or an indirect free kick. On a direct free kick you can shoot at goal. On an indirect free kick the ball must be passed to one of your team-mates before a shot at goal is taken. Players on the other team must be at least 10 yd (9.1 m) away from you for a free kick. England's David Beckham is one of the most famous free kickers of all time. He used to put lots of spin on the ball, often making it bend around defenders, past the goalkeeper, and into the goal.

1 The referee will point to where the foul took place and tell the kicker to take the free kick from there.

Tip

Keep your free kicks really simple. The more players you involve, and the more complicated you make them, the more likely they are to go wrong.

2 If it's a direct free kick and it's within scoring distance, the defending team should line up in a row (known as a wall) to block shots on goal. Players in the attacking team can stand in front of or near the wall, too, distracting the defenders and sometimes causing gaps in the wall.

3 Kick a free kick as you would a long kick (see page 30). If the defending team has lined up as a wall, you may choose to swerve the ball around the wall, or chip the ball over it.

Throw-ins

When a player from one team is the last to touch the ball before it goes past the touch line, the other team is given a throw-in.

1 Take the throw-in from the same place on the touch line that the ball left the pitch. Pick up the ball and stand with your feet behind the touch line.

2 Hold the ball right behind your head with both hands. Spread your hands around the back of the ball so that you can keep a firm grip on it during the throw.

3 When you're ready to throw the ball, arch your back and then push your chest forward while swinging both arms quickly forward over the top of your head. When you take the throw, both your feet must be on the ground, and both your hands must be on the ball.

Long throws

If your team is given a throw-in near the other team's goal, it's often a good idea to do a long throw into the penalty area to give your players a chance to shoot at goal.

Start your throw-in a few paces behind the touch line so that you have a run-up. This will give your throw extra momentum. Step forward, bringing the ball behind your head as you do so. Place your kicking leg near the touch line, keeping your non-kicking leg further back. Use the normal throw-in technique and follow right through. But make sure both feet are on the ground when you take the throw, and don't cross the touch line until you've released the ball.

4 Make sure you release the ball when it is directly above your head. Follow right through with both arms. You must not drop the ball directly down in front of you.

5 Try to throw the ball to the feet of an unmarked player on your team. Or throw the ball into a space where one of your team can run to it and get possession.

Handspring throw-ins

One way of getting extra-long distances on the throw-in is by doing something called a handspring (or somersault) throw-in.

This is one of the trickiest moves of all in soccer and should only be attempted by very experienced players. **You must only attempt this move if your coach is there and they agree that you can try it, as you could really hurt yourself.** The player takes a run-up and does a front handspring while holding the ball with both hands.

They then land on both feet and throw the ball with both hands—like a normal throw-in. The extra momentum from the run-up and the handspring gives the ball its distance.

Brazilian player Leah Fortune was one of the best female players at the handspring throw-in.

1   2   3

6 If you do a foul throw-in then the other team is given a throw-in instead. A foul throw is when you don't keep two feet on the ground, if you bring the ball in front of your head, or if you use just one hand to take the throw.

Penalties

If you like excitement and you like tension then you'll love penalty kicks. The referee will award a penalty if a defender does a foul in his or her own penalty area. Penalty kicks are never easy to take because there is so much pressure on the kicker to score a goal.

1 Place the ball on the penalty spot and walk a few paces back so that you have a run-up. Only you, the goalkeeper, and the referee are allowed in the penalty area until you have taken your kick.

Tip

Before you even start your run-up, decide what kind of penalty you're going to kick. Stick to your plan. If you change your mind halfway through, you risk missing the goal altogether.

2 Goalkeepers are allowed to wave their arms and move sideways along their goal line as you prepare to take your penalty. Don't be distracted by them. They are not allowed to move forward off their goal line before the ball is kicked

3 Once the referee blows the whistle you are allowed to take your penalty. Run up to the ball and kick it firmly in the direction you have decided on. For a more precise kick you can use the push pass kick (see page 28). For a harder kick you can use a long kick (see page 30). It's risky to aim high because the ball might fly over the top of the crossbar. It's much safer to kick the ball low and into one of the corners of the goal.

4 Other players—both attackers and defenders—should be ready in case the ball rebounds (bounces back) off the goalkeeper or the goalposts. Once the kick has been taken they can run into the penalty area and play a rebounded ball. The penalty kicker must wait until another player touches the ball before they can kick it again.

Shootouts

If you're playing in a knockout soccer competition, and your match ends in a draw after extra time, you may have to take part in a penalty shootout. Don't worry. This might be the most exciting part of the whole match!

Different competitions will have different types of shootouts but most see five players on each side taking turns to kick a penalty each. If both teams are still level after all 10 penalties have been taken, then more players take turns to kick penalties until one team goes a goal ahead.

chapter 3
Soccer skills
& drills

Heading the ball

A lot of young players are afraid of heading the ball because they think it will hurt. But it only hurts if you don't do it properly. Always try to head the ball with the middle of your forehead—the most solid part of your skull. Anywhere else and you won't be as accurate, and it may hurt. The best thing about heading is that you can control the ball before it reaches the ground and before an opposing player has time to get their feet to it.

Defensive header Defenders often use this type of header to clear a ball from their end of the field, away from the danger zone. Ideally you want to head the ball back down the field, high and long-distance. Or, if you're under pressure, it might be better to head the ball into the touch line for a throw-in or behind the goal line for a corner.

1 When you see a high ball coming toward you, get into position beneath where it's going to land. Plant your feet solidly on the ground, one foot behind the other. Keep your eyes on the ball as it comes toward you.

Safety

Always try to keep your eyes open as you head the ball (easier said than done!). Keep your mouth shut, too, so you don't bang your teeth together.

2 Bend your knees and, just as the ball drops down toward you, push up and forward to meet it with your forehead. Aim to head it halfway between the base and the middle of the ball.

3 Use the muscles in your neck to punch through the ball.

Attacking header On average, one in five goals in soccer are scored from headers. With an attacking header you are changing the direction of the ball so you need to put lots of force into it.

 1 If you're near the other team's goal and you see a high ball coming toward you, run toward it, keeping your eyes on it the whole time.

2 Jump up and forward to intercept the ball in mid-air. You'll need perfect timing for this.

3 Use your whole body, especially your legs and neck, to direct the ball with your head. To put even more power into it, arch your back and push your elbows backward as you lean your head and body forward to head the ball.

4 Because you want the ball to go into the goal, you will normally need to make contact with it higher than you would with a defensive header—somewhere between the middle and the top of the ball. This will stop the ball flying over the top of the crossbar.

Cushioned header Cushioned headers are used to pass the ball to team-mates. To give them the best chance to control the ball, you need to head the ball much more slowly, down to their feet. Instead of using your neck muscles to head the ball hard, you relax your neck muscles and pull your head back slightly on impact. This takes the pace (speed) out of the ball and drops it gently at their feet.

A cushioned header is also really useful when a defender is passing back to his goalkeeper because there's no risk that he'll miss it and let in an own goal. Goalkeepers aren't allowed to handle the ball if a defender kicks a ball back to them, but they are allowed if the ball is headed back to them.

Glancing header

These kinds of headers are used when you don't need to change the direction of the ball very much. They're great for scoring goals or passing the ball to a team-mate near you. You don't generate much power with a glancing header—you use the momentum that the ball already has and you deflect the ball with your forehead in another direction.

Volleying

Volleying is when you kick the ball while it's still in the air. Because you're not taking time to control the ball, you can easily catch defenders and goalkeepers unaware. The element of surprise will be with you. You need perfect timing for a volley but with a bit of practice you'll soon get the hang of it. If you connect cleanly with the ball it can make for a really impressive goal.

Volleys from the side This is when you're in front of the other team's goal and a high cross comes toward you from the wing.

1 Watch the ball really carefully as it comes toward you.

2 Lean back slightly and raise your kicking foot, ready to connect with the ball. Use your arms to keep yourself balanced. Your other leg remains on the ground.

3 Swing your kicking leg round hard and fast, kicking the ball with the top of your boot. Rotate your whole body round as you do this, twisting your non-kicking leg, too.

4 Follow through downward with your leg so that the ball stays low and doesn't fly over the top of the goal.

Goalkeeping

It's not easy being a goalkeeper. It's a stressful position to play in soccer—probably the most stressful on the whole pitch. Make a mistake and everyone is watching. On the other hand, make a great save and the rest of your team will love you.

Most goalkeepers are tall with big hands. They are also agile, strong, and not afraid to dive on the ball or get kicked by players from the other team. From their position at the back of the pitch, they should be smart and confident in telling their defenders what to do. They should also be good at kicking the ball long distances.

Tip

All goalkeepers need a really good pair of goalkeeping gloves (see page 11).

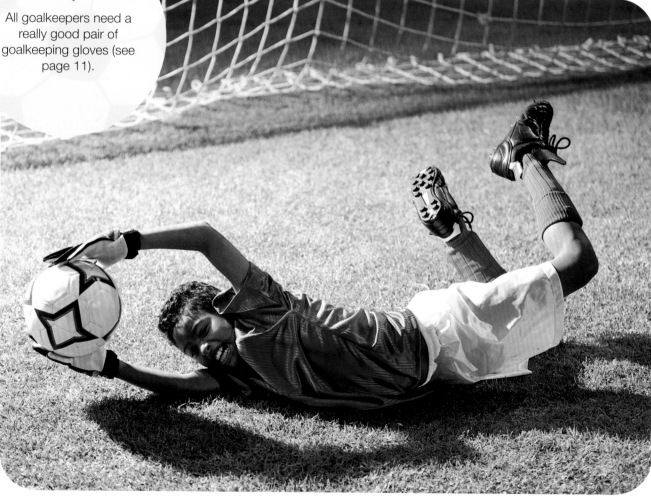

Basic goalkeeping skills

Learn these basic skills and you will be a solid last line of defense for your team.

Position Goalkeepers must always be ready to leap into action, even when they least expect it. Even if the play is all the way up the other end of the pitch, and the other team's strikers never get through the defense, it's no good just hanging out on your goal line. You must be ready to take part at all times.

 When you see the play coming toward you, it's important to stand the right way—your legs shoulder-width apart, your body slightly forward, with your weight on your toes and your arms in front of you.

2 Keep watching the ball, even if it's a long way from your goal. Place yourself in between the ball and your goal mouth, ready for a surprise shot.

3 If you move across your goal mouth, use side steps so that you're always facing the ball.

4 Good goalkeepers will shout instructions to their defenders, pointing out where strikers might attack. On direct free kicks and corners, the goalkeeper should direct other players, telling them where to stand and who to mark. The goalkeeper is also allowed to throw the ball back into play.

Chest catches

On easy saves, goalkeepers need to catch the ball and make it safe. If the ball is coming toward you, bouncing along the ground, then a chest catch is normally the best option.

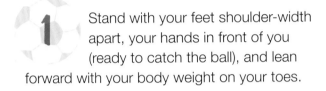

Stand with your feet shoulder-width apart, your hands in front of you (ready to catch the ball), and lean forward with your body weight on your toes.

Watch the ball carefully as it comes toward you.

3 Using little side steps, move your body so that your chest is fully behind the ball when it reaches you.

4 Lean forward and bend your knees as the ball comes toward your hands. This will absorb the power of the shot. Your hands should be in front of your chest in the shape of a W.

5 Catch the ball, bring it in toward your chest, and fold your arms around it so it can't fall onto the pitch. If you feel yourself falling forward, land gently on your knees. Keep the ball safe.

Low stops

Often, a shot on goal will roll along the ground toward you. It may look simple to stop but you still need to concentrate. If you don't, it's easy to let in a goal through your hands or legs.

• Watch the ball carefully as it comes toward you and use little side steps to put yourself in its path.

• Kneel down on one knee so that your knee makes a barrier with the heel of your other foot. Spread both hands wide, catch the ball, and pull it safely toward your chest.

Distributing the ball

Once goalkeepers have safely gathered the ball they then need to distribute it back to their players. They might throw it (for short distances) or kick it (for longer distances).

Rolling the ball Sometimes, rolling the ball out to one of your players is much better and more accurate than kicking it. Especially if your player isn't far away.

Hold the ball in the palm of your strongest hand and roll it underarm along the ground, right to your player's feet.

Drop down onto one knee and follow right through to give the ball power.

Overarm throws Overarm throws will go much further than underarm throws. But remember they will bounce. You need to be careful to keep them accurate, and not let an attacking player intercept your throw.

Hold the ball in your strongest hand, back behind your head — as if you're giving someone a high five. Take a couple of strides and then throw the ball hard toward your team-mate's feet. Follow right through to give the ball some power.

Goal kick All goalkeepers need to take good, strong goal kicks. Practice these a lot so, come match time, they are second nature to you. All attacking players must be outside your penalty area when you take a goal kick. Your defenders can stay in the penalty area if you want, but they can't touch the ball until it has left the penalty area.

You can kick a goal kick from anywhere in your goal area, but most goalkeepers place it on the front line of the goal area.

Take several paces as a run-up and then kick the ball either with the top of your boot or the inside of your toes. Aim to kick the ball at one of your unmarked team-mates. Follow right through with your kicking foot to give the ball some power.

Punt or drop kick Once you have made the ball safe, you can kick it out to one of your team-mates. A punt (kicking the ball before it bounces on the ground) or a drop kick (bouncing the ball on the ground before you kick it) are really good ways to send the ball a long distance.

Quick check

Make sure there are no attacking players nearby before you take a punt or a drop kick, just in case they try to steal the ball from you when you let it out of your hands.

1 For both kicks, hold the ball in both hands and take a couple of paces as a run-up. For the punt, drop the ball onto your kicking foot just as you swing your leg forward.

2 For a drop kick, drop the ball onto the ground first and then kick it. On both kicks, kick the ball with the top of your boot, and follow right through (keep your leg moving) to get lots of power.

Back pass rule Any time a throw-in or an intentional back pass (when the ball is passed deliberately) comes to you from one of your team-mates, you're not allowed to use your hands, otherwise the other team will get a free kick. Instead you must use your feet.

Don't take any risks on a back pass. Kick the ball back to your team-mates as quickly as you can. If attacking players are bearing down on you, there's nothing wrong with playing safe and kicking the ball straight into touch (out of play and over the edge of the pitch, beyond the touch line).

Making saves Goalkeepers need to be ready to leap into action at any moment. They must jump, dive, punch, and catch—whatever is needed to stop the ball going in the goal.

Catching saves Sometimes you'll have to dive to stop the ball, but it will be close enough to your body that you can catch it. Watch the ball carefully and dive toward it, using your nearest leg to push off. Try to get your chest right behind it. Your hands should be in the shape of a W before you catch the ball.

Once you've caught it, bring the ball close to your chest and fold your arms around it. If you land on your shoulder this will cushion your fall.

Diving saves Goalkeepers often have to stretch wide to make a save. In this case they'll have no chance of catching the ball. Their only option is to deflect it or push it away.

Always try to get two hands to the ball, even when you're stretching right out to the goalpost. If you can, push the ball away from the goal with the palms of your hands. Otherwise just get one hand to the ball and deflect it from going into the goal. Try to make sure the ball doesn't end up going straight back to an attacking player.

Get back on your feet as quickly as possible in case you have to make another save.

High catches Goalkeepers can reach much higher than other players because they can stretch their arms up to catch a high ball. If an attacking player kicks a high cross into your penalty area, sometimes it's worth running forward to catch the ball before another player makes a header or a shot on goal.

Once you've made your decision to catch the ball, stick to it. Run forward and jump off one foot to get as much height as possible. Catch the ball high, above where attacking players can head it.

If you're not sure you can catch the ball then you should punch it away instead. Punch it hard, away from your goal and toward the sides of the pitch.

Narrow the angle Sometimes an attacking player will break through your defenders and run toward your goal. If you stay on your goal line, they will have most of the goal mouth to aim for. It is much better if you run out toward the attacker because this will cut down the angles and give them less space to aim for.

Make your body as big as possible by waving your arms and spreading your legs. This will help block any shots and it might distract the attacking player.

Tip over the bar Some of the most difficult shots to save are high ones, into the corner of your goal. You may not be able to catch the ball in these situations. Sometimes it's much better to tip the ball back over the crossbar, for a corner kick.

It's very difficult to control these high shots, so don't try to stop the ball and catch it, otherwise you risk giving it away to an attacking player who will of course take another shot at goal. It is much better to give away a corner instead of risking a goal.

Practice drills and games

There's only one way to get good at soccer—and that's to keep practicing. Practice drills are great fun, especially if you turn them into a game with other players. And they're perfect if you don't have enough time for a full match.
All professional soccer players do practice drills.

Soccer tag This game is just like playground tag, except that all the players have to dribble balls while playing it.

Every player tucks a spare T-shirt into the back of their shorts. They then dribble their ball around the pitch while trying to snatch as many T-shirts as possible from other players. But they have to keep control of their ball at all times. The winner is the player who snatches the most T-shirts and keeps control of their ball.

Juggling Three or more players stand in a large circle. Using their feet, knees, or heads, they try to volley the ball in the air, passing it to each other on each volley. One bounce is allowed, but more than one bounce will result in a forfeit (maybe 5 push-ups). Players also get forfeits if they do a bad volley pass or if they miss an easy ball.

Header practice Three or more players stand in a large circle around one player in the middle. The player in the middle throws the ball underhand at a random player on the outside, yelling "head" or "catch" as they do so. But here's the trick: if the player in the middle yells "catch" then the player must head the ball back to them; if they yell "head," then the player must catch the ball.

It's easy to get **CONFUSED** in this game!

Dribble and shoot Set up five or six cones—each 4 ft (1.2 m) apart—in a line stretching toward the goal. Each player must then slalom dribble around the cones before shooting at the goal.

Hat-trick Players take it in turns to shoot at goal. For their first shot they must kick a dead ball from the penalty spot. For their second shot they must control or trap a ball passed to them from the side—and then shoot at goal. For their third shot they must kick a moving ball passed to them from the side—and volley it into the goal.

Pirate treasure First you must set up a line of 10 cones on the touch line. This is the treasure. Three players are the pirates—it's their job to defend the treasure. The rest of the players line up with a ball each and try to dribble around the pirates and knock over the cones by kicking their balls at them. Of course, the pirates defend their cones by tackling the other players.

The game finishes once all the cones have been knocked over.

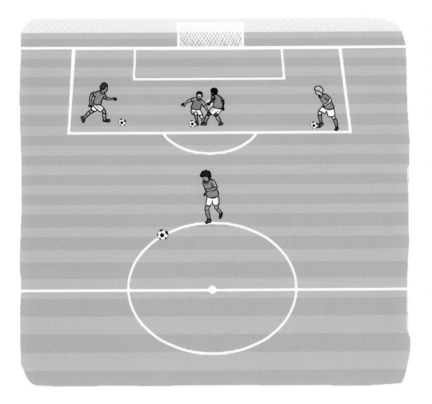

Clean your room Four players dribble a ball each around inside the penalty area. One player (the room cleaner) has to tackle each player in turn, win the ball, and kick it as hard and far as possible out of the area.

The player who lost his or her ball must then quickly run and retrieve it while the room cleaner carries on tackling other players and kicking their balls out of the area.

The room is clean when all four balls are out of the area at the same time.

Space invaders One player starts in the middle of the pitch with a ball. (He or she is the defender.) The other players double up into teams of two, holding hands at all times. (They are the space invaders.)

The defender then tries to tag the space invaders by kicking the ball at them (below knee height otherwise someone might get hurt!). The space invaders can run around but they must continue holding hands at all times. Once a team of space invaders gets tagged, they join the defender in the middle and help them to pick off the remaining space invaders.

Three and in This game is great for practicing goal scoring and goalkeeping. And you can play it with as few as three players.

One player starts off as goalkeeper while the other players all compete as one-person teams, tackling each other and trying to score whenever possible.

Once one player has completed a hat-trick (three goals), he or she then swaps with the goalkeeper. Everyone gets a turn at scoring and saving goals.

Long passing Only two of you? Here's a great game to practice your passing skills. Start off by standing 15 ft (4.5 m) apart. Kick long passes to each other, moving back 5 ft (1.5 m) after you've completed each pass.

Eventually you'll end up about 50 ft (15 m) apart. Try to place the ball at your friend's feet on each pass.

Coach's revenge

The coach stands in the middle of the pitch with a large supply of soccer balls. Players must then sprint across the pitch and avoid being touched by the balls that the coach kicks at them (below knee height or someone might get hurt!). Once they're touched by a ball, players must join the coach in the middle of the pitch and try to tag the remaining players. The winner is the last player to be tagged.

Soccer tricks

Trick shots and special moves look really impressive if you practice them and get them right. But they look really silly if you get them wrong. It's probably best not to use them in a match unless you are 100 percent confident.

Keepy-uppies Everyone loves doing keepy-uppies. The idea is that you try to bounce or juggle the ball as many times as you can non-stop on your feet, on the top of your thighs (or even your head, if you're good enough). If the ball bounces on the ground then you have to start again.

For beginners, any more than 10 keepy-uppies in a row is really good. Professional players can do it hundreds of times without letting the ball bounce on the ground. One English player once did keepy-uppies for 26 hours, without the ball touching the ground once. That's amazing!

Balance the ball on your back This trick looks really cool but you'll never need to use it during an actual match.

 Start with the ball balanced on your forehead. Tilt your head back so it doesn't fall off.

2 With your forehead, nudge the ball straight up into the air. Then immediately drop your head forward, allowing the ball to fall directly downward.

3 Now your shoulder blades will be directly beneath the ball. Arch your back and push your elbows upward. This creates a dip for the ball to land in. With any luck, the ball will stay there.

Back flick This trick is a lot easier than it looks. Stand with one foot forward and one foot back, and place the ball between the heel of your front foot and the toes of your back foot.

Gently start to roll the ball up the heel of your front foot using the toes of your back foot. When the ball is slightly off the ground, suddenly flick your heel backward so that the ball jumps straight up and over the back of your head.

The step-over This is a great trick to use when you're dribbling toward the goal and a defender tries to tackle you.

1 As you're dribbling along, pretend to play the ball with the outside of your left foot. The defender will move sideways to follow you.

2 At the last minute, step all the way over the ball with your left foot.

3 Now use the outside of your right foot to play the ball instead.

4 Move to the right, taking the ball with you and avoiding the defender altogether.

The drag back or pull back Here's a great trick to use when a defender is trying to tackle you.

1 Swing your kicking leg toward the ball as if you're going to kick it. Stop just before you kick, and place your kicking foot on top of the ball.

2 In one smooth movement, use the studs on your boot to drag the ball backward and behind you.

3 Now use the same foot to push the ball forward again but in another direction.

4 Hopefully you'll have confused the defender so that you can run off in another direction without getting tackled.

The Cruyff Turn Back in the 1970s there was a very famous Dutch soccer player called Johan Cruyff. He was the world expert at tricking defenders with a dummy and a turn. It became known as the Cruyff Turn, and it's still known as that today.

1 Swing your kicking leg toward the ball as if you're going to kick it.

2 Instead of kicking the ball, bring your kicking foot over the top of the ball.

3 Use the inside of your kicking foot to flick the ball back between your legs, in the opposite direction that the defender was expecting.

4 Twist your body and run after the ball, away from the defender, in the opposite direction.

Overhead kick This is one of the trickiest shots of all in soccer because your timing has to be absolutely perfect. But, get it right, and you will be a team hero. It's sometimes called the bicycle kick.

 1 When you see the ball coming toward you, face away from the goal. Lean your body back, and put your weight onto your kicking foot.

 2 Watching the ball really carefully, lean even further backward and stretch out your arms.

 3 Bring your non-kicking leg up into the air.

4 At the last moment, bring your kicking leg up sharp and fast. Try to connect with the ball when your body is parallel to the ground.

Warning

Never do this trick on a hard pitch or you risk hurting your back and head. Only ever do it when you have very soft grass, sand, or a mat to land on. Make sure your coach is with you when you try it.

5 Bring your kicking leg right over your body toward your head. This will keep the ball low, and stop you kicking it over the crossbar.

6 Use your arms and non-kicking leg to cushion your fall when you hit the ground. Be really careful you don't land directly on your back or your backside—and be extra careful not to bang your head on the ground.

chapter 4
Tactics– playing to win

Formations

In a proper game of soccer, every player plays in a certain position. Defenders and the goalkeeper play at the back, wingers play on the wing, strikers attack the goal, and midfielders move between the back and the front. Imagine what chaos it would be if no one played in their proper position and just chased the ball the whole time!

But some teams are more attacking while others are more defensive. That's because different teams use different formations. Like armies, they might choose to put more of their players at the front, or more at the back.

Here are some common team formations. Professional soccer players describe them by using the number of players in each part of the pitch, starting with the defenders and moving forward. (Goalkeepers aren't included.) So, 4-4-2 means four defenders (at the back), four midfielders (in the center), and two forwards (at the front). 4-3-3 means four defenders, three midfielders, and three forwards.

In the junior game, team coaches will decide which formation is best for their team.

Keep it flexible

In the professional game, team managers change their team formations depending on who they're playing or where their strengths and weaknesses are. Sometimes they switch formations halfway through a match, depending on whether they're winning or losing.

Left back   Left midfield

Center back   Center midfield   Center forward

Center back   Center midfield   Center forward

Right back   Right midfield

4-4-2

A barrier of four defenders and four midfielders make it very difficult for the opposition to score. The two forwards must work hard to get goal-scoring chances.

This formation is very popular with British teams.

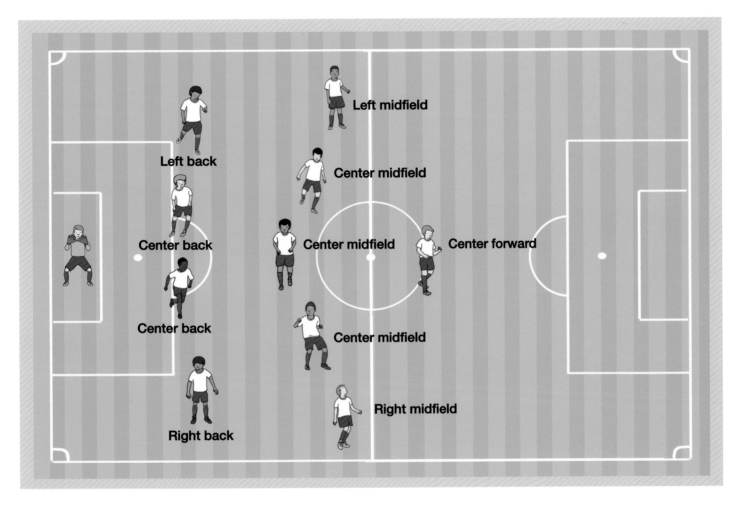

4-5-1

This is a very defensive formation, giving the
opposition very few chances to score. However,
with only one striker up front, it offers very few
attacking chances.

This formation is popular with European teams.

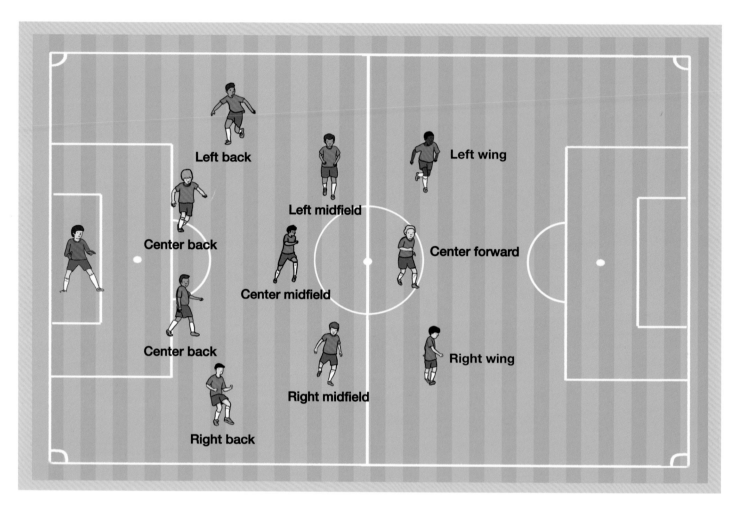

Left back

Left midfield

Left wing

Center back

Center forward

Center midfield

Center back

Right wing

Right midfield

Right back

4-3-3

This formation is much more attacking, with the three forwards spread across the pitch, always threatening the opposition's goal.

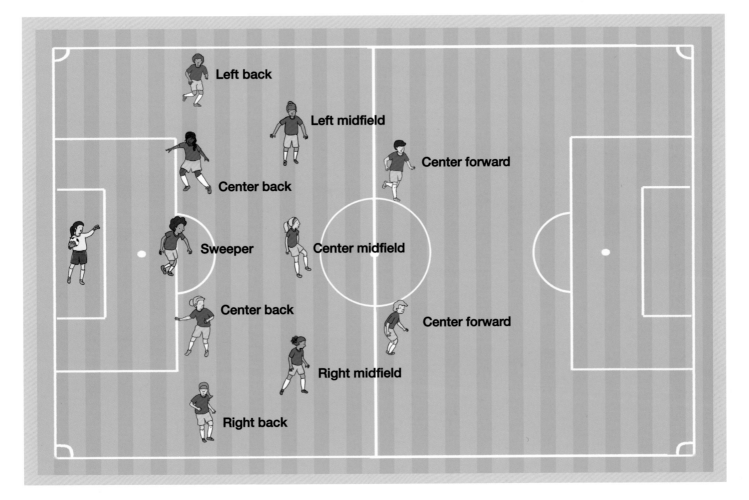

Left back

Left midfield

Center forward

Center back

Sweeper

Center midfield

Center back

Center forward

Right midfield

Right back

5-3-2

With five defenders, this formation stops the opposition from scoring. But at the same time, the two wing-back defenders (on the left and right wings) can easily move up the pitch in attack. They need to be really fit so they can run all the way forward or all the way back when they're needed. A sweeper is a defender who "sweeps" up the ball when attackers break the defensive line.

Attacking tactics

Never forget that soccer is a team sport. You will win more
matches if you all play together as an 11-person team, instead of
as lots of individuals.

Lose your marker It's no good getting the ball if
you're surrounded by players from the other team.
If you want your team-mates to pass to you, move
into a space, away from players who are marking
you. Then, once you receive the ball, you'll have
more time and more choices for your next move.

Support your team-mates When team-mates make an attack on the opposition's goal, don't let them run off on their own. You should follow close to them so that they can pass to you if they get in trouble. Call out to them so that they know you are nearby.

Use the width of the pitch Most defenders stay in the middle of the pitch, protecting their goal. When you're attacking, it's a good idea to use the whole width of the pitch, right out toward the wings on each side. This way, attackers can either draw defenders out wide, away from the goal, or they can make crosses to their own players in the middle.

Wall passes Dribbling past an opponent can be very tricky. Sometimes it's much better to do a move called a wall pass (or a one-two pass).

As you dribble toward an opponent, just before you reach them, make a little pass to a team-mate at the side, then run past the opponent. Your team-mate should then pass the ball straight back to you once you're the other side of the opponent. It's called a wall pass because it would be the same as if you kicked the ball against a wall and waited for it to bounce back to you.

The counter attack Counter attack is when you suddenly turn defense into attack. It's really effective because the opposition isn't expecting it and will be taken by surprise.

Here's a great way to counter attack: if the goalkeeper or a defender has the ball and lots of attackers are bearing down on them, he or she should kick a really long pass upfield to one of their own attackers. But the kick needs to be done suddenly—and out of the blue—so that the attacking players don't have time to get themselves in a defensive position.

Once the goalkeeper or defender makes the pass, their team-mates should follow up in attack.

Defending tactics

It's impossible to stop the opposition from scoring if you don't all play together as a defending unit. That means lots of organization and tactics.

Zonal marking Instead of sticking to one attacker, defenders are sometimes given an area of their half of the field to patrol. They then mark any attacker who strays into their area. When the attacker leaves their area, another defender takes over marking duties.

Marking Marking—or staying close to another player—is the key to good defense. Each defender is given an attacker from the opposing team to mark. It's then his or her job to be aware of what that attacker is doing at all times, and to stick close to them like glue. Any time the ball comes to that attacker, the defender can either steal the ball from them or kick it away safely.

When marking, it's safest to place yourself between the attacking player and your own goal. This stops them attacking your goal.

Tackling All defenders have to tackle attacking players to stop them getting close to the goal and taking a shot. For tackling skills, see page 46.

Intercepting passes If one of your defenders is about to tackle an attacker from the other team, that attacker may feel pressure to pass the ball to one of their team-mates. If you think and move quickly, you can intercept the ball while it rolls from the passer to the receiver.

Make sure you can definitely make the interception, though. If you miss the ball then the attacking player who receives it might have a clear run at goal.

Clearances It's great if defenders can kick a long ball up to one of their own team-mates further up the pitch. But often defenders don't have time for this because attackers are running at them really quickly. In these situations it's always better to play safe by taking a big, long kick upfield, or by kicking the ball into touch (over the touch line). These kicks are called clearances.

Defending corner kicks Defenders must be really alert whenever the other team takes a corner kick. As the kicker prepares to take the kick, defenders must each mark an attacking player, moving as they move, and staying between that player and their own goal.

There should also be one defender on each goal post to help the goalkeeper by kicking away shots that are played to the sides of the goal.

Defending free kicks If the opposing team has a direct free kick, it's a good idea for the defense to form a wall. Normally the goalkeeper will be in charge of where the wall should stand (see page 52).

The defenders must stand firm, without moving, in the wall. They must never let a free kick pass through the wall.

Offside trap To carry out the offside trap, defenders need to be playing as a tight unit, working together. Communication is essential. One defender should take responsibility for organizing the offside trap.

This is how it works: the defenders stand in a line between the attackers and their own goal. When they see one attacker about to pass the ball to another attacker who is running forward, they all step forward as a single line so that the running attacker is caught offside (see page 18).

But remember that if one defender forgets to step forward, the running attacker won't be offside and could break through to score a goal. That would be a disaster.

Soccer rules quiz

So, you think you know the rules of soccer? Reckon you could give the referee a run for his money? Why not try yourself at our quiz on the rules of the game?
See page 110 for the answers.

1 A defender takes a throw-in and decides to play it safe by throwing the ball straight back to his or her goalkeeper. But, oh no! The goalkeeper isn't paying attention. They don't see the ball which rolls straight into the net. What happens?

A The goal counts. It's an own goal.
B Another throw-in must be taken.
C The other team gets to take a corner kick.

2 Before entering the field of play, a substitute does the following things. Which one is allowed?

A They take a corner kick.
B They take a free kick.
C They take a throw-in.

3 Goalkeepers have to be careful about the kit they wear. Which of the following are they not allowed to do?

A Roll down their socks.
B Wear headbands.
C Roll up their sleeves.

4 A defender takes a huge kick upfield. Ouch! The ball hits the referee and bounces back into the defender's own goal. What happens?

A A penalty for the attacking team.
B A drop ball.
C The goal counts.

5 A striker kicks the ball at goal. The ball hits the crossbar and bounces down straight onto the goal line, in the middle of the goal mouth. What happens?

A Play continues.
B A goal is awarded.
C The attacking team takes a corner kick.

6 When taking throw-ins, what are players NOT allowed to do?

A Throw the ball to their own goalkeeper.
B Throw the ball straight into the other team's goal.
C Throw the ball with just one hand.

7 The goalkeeper runs up to take a goal kick. At the very last minute an attacking player runs into the penalty area and intercepts the ball. What happens?

A The goal kick must be taken again.
B The goalkeeper gets a free kick.
C Play continues.

8 At the start of the match, on kick-off, a player kicks the ball really hard straight into the goal. What happens?

A The goal is given.
B The other team is given a free kick.
C The player who scored must take the kick-off again.

Resources

Useful organizations

US Soccer:
www.ussoccer.com

US Youth Soccer:
www.usyouthsoccer.org

Answers to Soccer rules quiz, pages 108–109

1. Answer C.
2. Answer B.
3. Answer C, because the referee must be able to see who is handling the ball in a large group of players.
4. Answer C because, like other players and goalposts, referees are seen as a normal part of the game. If the ball hits them, play continues.
5. Answer A. The whole of the ball must cross the goal line for a goal to count.
6. Answer C.
7. Answer A.
8. Answer A.

Index